99 Ways
to Increase
Your Income

D1456869

99 Ways to Increase Your Income

Frank Martin

WATERBROOK
PRESS

99 WAYS TO INCREASE YOUR INCOME
PUBLISHED BY WATERBROOK PRESS
12265 Oracle Boulevard, Suite 200
Colorado Springs, Colorado 80921

The Scripture in the Introduction and in epigraphs for chapters 1, 3, 5, and 7 are from The Message by Eugene H. Peterson. Copyright © 1993, 1994, 1995, 1996, 2000, 2001, 2002. Used by permission of NavPress Publishing Group. All rights reserved. Scripture epigraph for chapter 2 is taken from the Contemporary English Version. Copyright © 1991, 1992, 1995 by American Bible Society. Used by permission. Scripture epigraphs for chapters 4 and 6 are taken from the Holy Bible, New International Version®. NIV®. Copyright © 1973, 1978, 1984 by International Bible Society. Used by permission of Zondervan Publishing House. All rights reserved.

ISBN 978-0-307-45839-1
ISBN 978-0-307-45845-2 (electronic)

Published in the United States by WaterBrook Multnomah, an imprint of the Crown Publishing Group, a division of Random House Inc., New York.

WATERBROOK and its deer colophon are registered trademarks of Random House Inc.

Library of Congress Cataloging-in-Publication Data
Martin, Frank, 1958–
    99 ways to increase your income / Frank Martin.—1st ed.
        p. cm.
    ISBN 978-0-307-45839-1—ISBN 978-0-307-45845-2 (electronic) 1. Finance, Personal. I. Title. II. Title: Ninety-nine ways to increase your income.
    HG179.M313 2009
    332.024'01—dc22

                                        2009012138

Printed in the United States of America
2009—First Edition

10 9 8 7 6 5 4 3 2 1

SPECIAL SALES
Most WaterBrook Multnomah books are available at special quantity discounts when purchased in bulk by corporations, organizations, and special-interest groups. Custom imprinting or excerpting can also be done to fit special needs. For information, please e-mail SpecialMarkets@WaterBrookMultnomah.com or call 1-800-603-7051.

Contents

Introduction

As a teenager I worked in a bakery, frying doughnuts for the morning customers. This meant I had to be at work by 3 a.m. Often I would drag in thirty minutes late, half-asleep and disheveled. My boss, Sandy, would shake his head and say, "You know, any old fool can go to bed at night, but it takes a real man to get up in the morning."

I must have heard that phrase a hundred times, but never really understood it until I went into business for myself. It's a principle as simple as it is timeless—one that every successful person has learned in one form or another. Knowing what you need to do and doing it are not the same things.

Almost all of us have a desire to earn extra income for our family or to at least make the best possible choices when it comes to money. We want to be wise about how we use our time, talents, and resources. We long for the day we can give more, worry less, and be financially independent. And we know that there are steps we need to follow in order to achieve those goals. As the Bible proverb advises, "Take good counsel and accept correction— that's the way to live wisely and well" (Proverbs 19:20).

If you want wisdom on finances, this little book just may be your first step toward doing what you know needs to be done in order to move forward. There are thousands of ways to increase your family income, but you need only a few of them to succeed. Included here are ninety-nine tried-and-true ideas to get you started. It's not an exhaustive list—just a few thoughts worth getting up in the morning for.

1 Foundations of Financial Management

> Get wisdom—it's worth more than money;
>
> choose insight over income every time.
>
> —PROVERBS 16:16

Any desire to earn extra income has to begin with a basic understanding of healthy financial management. No effort to make additional money will succeed if you haven't first learned to make wise choices with the resources you bring in. That's why we're devoting the first section of this book to the basics. It's the old "putting the horse before the cart" principle. Once you learn to walk, running comes naturally. But you do have to learn to walk first, and that may mean a few bumps and bruises along the way. Some of these ideas may seem elementary, but here's a promise from me to you: put these basic principles into practice and you'll be positioned to forever change your financial future.

1 ⟩ TAKE A FINANCIAL X-RAY

When a doctor needs to know what's going on inside your body, he takes an internal snapshot—an x-ray. This reveals hidden problems that don't always show up on the surface. It's often the first step in diagnosing a serious problem. Why not take that same approach with your finances? Begin by keeping track for an entire month of everything you spend—down to the last cup of coffee or package of gum. Be specific, accurate, and honest. Then create a personalized spreadsheet so that you have a detailed overview of your monthly income and expenses—just like a company's profit-and-loss statement. This is your financial x-ray in black and white. It's your most important diagnostic tool. If your outgo exceeds your income, you have a serious problem. And the next step is to plot out a plan to fix it.

2 ⟩ WRITE OUT A BUDGET

Let's face it: life is more fun without a budget. A budget is your financial dorm mother telling you what you can and can't do. It sets perimeters on your buying and spending habits that you'd rather not have. But the truth is, we all need them. Budgets are our tether to reality. And in the world of getting ahead, they serve as an invaluable road map to financial freedom. Use the financial x-ray you took as a tool for creating a written monthly budget. Now that you can see at a glance where your money is going, make tough decisions about where to make needed cuts. Your goal is to do more than simply balance the budget but also to identify and eliminate wasteful spending habits. Remember, you want to get ahead, not just break even. Set a budget that allows you a profit at the end of each month—money left over to save and invest.

3 HAVE WRITTEN GOALS

Think about how you plan a long road trip. You start with a road map, placing one finger where you are and the other where you want to go. Then you plot out the best way to get there, breaking it down into small, manageable increments. Use that same principle with your financial goals. Do you want to earn an extra $10,000 this year? Pay off a car early? Save money to start a business? Decide where you want to go; then write out a detailed map to help you get there. Include specific dates and time lines to help keep you on track. Flesh it out as clearly as possible. Then stick to your plan. Studies show that only 2 percent of people actually set written goals for financial success, but those who do almost always get where they're going.

4 NARROW YOUR OBJECTIVES

When setting your financial goals, it's important to identify the ones that matter most so that those objectives go to the top of your priority list. For instance, is early retirement your number-one priority? If so, that should take the top spot. Do you want to make sure you have enough to send your kids to a good college? Jot it down. Are you worried about job security? Then a healthy emergency fund needs to be a top priority. List your priorities in order of importance, then begin by focusing on the top three. When those objectives are met, you can move on to the next three. This is how successful businesses decide where to focus their energies, and it's a good approach to personal finances as well. This way you remain focused and always have a specific financial goal you are working toward.

5 > PRIORITY #1: GET OUT OF DEBT

Any financial plan should begin with a goal to get out of debt—first and foremost. There's no easy formula. Falling into debt is always easier than digging out of it. But here are a few tried-and-true steps to get you started. First, order your debts from the lowest to the highest balance, then decide how much money you can pay toward these debts each month. The more disciplined you are, the faster you'll be free. Then continue paying the minimum balance on all the debts except the one with the lowest balance. That one you commit to paying as much as you possibly can each month until it is paid in full. Then take on the next lowest debt and do the same thing, without altering the monthly amount you pay. Use this formula and you'll be debt free far sooner than you might expect.

6 > AUTOMATE YOUR BILLS

Discipline is essential to financial freedom, and one of the fastest ways to learn discipline is to automate your routine monthly transactions. When you do this, you remove the temptation to spend money in your account that needs to go toward bills. You also remove the human element, making it more difficult to mess things up. Start moving toward a system of paperless bill paying by setting up your regular bills to draft right out of your account—things like utilities, phone bills, even your house payment. You can also set up automatic drafts to your savings and retirement accounts. Then your job becomes as simple as making sure you deposit your funds on time while keeping an eye on your account so that the payments don't bounce. The discipline you'll learn will be helpful in every area of life, not just finances.

7 SET REALISTIC EXPECTATIONS

The reason most families get into debt over their heads is really quite simple. The average person's salary increases between 2.5 percent and 3.5 percent per year. Because of this, many people anticipate having more money in the future than they have now. They take on extra debt assuming that they'll be fine the next year when their promotion kicks in or they get their annual bonus. But that kind of thinking needs to change—especially in an ailing economy. The smart approach is to expect the best but prepare for the worst. If you get a raise, use the extra money to pay bills down or to increase your emergency fund. And do the same with annual bonuses or tax refunds. If you assume you'll be making more money, you will spend it; however, if you acknowledge that your prosperity could end at any time, you will save it.

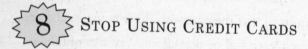

8 › STOP USING CREDIT CARDS

This may seem like a no-brainer, but if you've found yourself deep in debt, it's probably because you keep using credit. The cure is to break the habit. Decide today to put away your credit cards and stop using them. Cut them up if you have to, but don't carry them with you. The truth is, credit cards are debt traps. And the excuses people give for having them seldom hold water. They're not good safety nets, and the mileage or cash-back rewards you earn by using them are just ploys to get you to spend more money. If you're serious about getting out of debt, the first step is to put away your cards and pay as you go.

9   USE A DEBIT CARD TO TRACK EXPENSES

Some financial experts encourage people to use only cash when working toward debt-free living, but I think a better approach is to start using a debit card tied to your primary bank account—one that you can view online and track regularly. Many banks offer free checking with free online services. This way you can track your expenses for tax purposes. It's also a good log of your spending habits for future reference. Just make sure to keep an eye on your account so you don't overspend. Get into the habit of logging each transaction in your checkbook, just as you would if you'd written a check. And balance it at the end of each week, just to make sure you're staying on budget.

10   ESTABLISH AN EMERGENCY FUND

This may seem counterintuitive. *I thought the idea was to pay off debts first?* you may ask. It is, but without a buffer, unexpected expenses can easily turn into a disaster. We recently took our van into the shop for a simple brake adjustment and learned that the transmission was about to go. We had to have it replaced. The final bill came to just over $3,500. The cost was completely unexpected, and it was tempting to put it on a card and deal with it later. But we instead used our emergency fund, then spent the following months paying back the fund. If you've put away your credit cards for good, an emergency fund is critical, just in case you need it. How much you need depends on your situation, but a good rule of thumb is three to six months' salary.

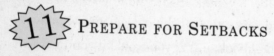 PREPARE FOR SETBACKS

Any time you set out to achieve a goal or carry out a plan, you have to expect setbacks. It's part of being human. Whenever I set out to lose ten or twenty pounds, the first few days go rather well. There's an excitement about the idea of being thinner, so I start dropping weight right away. But along the way my resolve starts to wear thin. I begin to crave doughnuts and chocolate, and sometimes I give in and cheat. It's tempting to give up, even though I know that if I stay the course and do the right things the weight will eventually come off. The same is true with finances. Setbacks will happen. The dishwasher will break down, the kids will need braces, something will happen to temporarily derail your plan. But resolve to stay the course, no matter what.

12 DEVELOP A FRUGAL MIND-SET

There's an interesting dynamic that happens whenever people start to dig themselves out of debt. They tend to forget what it was like being burdened with monthly bills and start reverting to old spending habits. I've seen it happen time and again. But true financial freedom only comes when we develop a new way of thinking—a frugal mind-set. You have to change the way you look at money. Instead of focusing on things you think you need—like a new car or an updated wardrobe—think of the additional freedom that money can buy down the road. Imagine yourself retiring a year earlier or enjoying that Alaskan cruise you and your spouse plan to take on your thirtieth anniversary. Delayed gratification can be more exciting than spending if you know how to focus your thoughts properly.

{13} BECOME A SAVINGS ADDICT

Once people have experienced the joy of true financial independence, they can't imagine going back to living paycheck to paycheck. The thought of spending money feels painful to them. I have a friend who retired at the age of forty-four with enough savings and investments to last the rest of his life. Yet you'd never catch him spending $4 on a cup of coffee. He recently lost his three-year-old cell phone, and instead of buying a new one from his provider, he found one on eBay for $15. He hates spending money but loves shuffling CDs and money-market accounts from one bank to another in order to get a better interest rate. He's addicted to saving and investing, simply because he's felt the freedom it brings. Ultimately, that should be the goal of anyone serious about becoming financially secure.

{14} PRACTICE GENEROSITY

This entry may be last for this section, but in my mind it is first in importance. No financial plan should be put into practice without first determining how much you can give to others. Generosity is not something you do; it's an extension of who you are. And those who give, even during the lean times, are saying to themselves and others, "No matter how little I have, I will always do my part to help those less fortunate, because I trust that there will always be more." A generous spirit is a loving spirit, and love always returns more than it gives. As a Christian, I give because I see it as a biblical principle. But that's not the primary reason. I choose to be generous because giving reminds me to practice selflessness in all I do. Giving brings pleasure and blessing far more satisfying than riches.

Putting Your Plan into Action

Once you learn the basics of healthy financial management, you're on your way to creating new and exciting streams of income. But knowing these principles is just the first step. You have to proactively work at putting your plan into motion. Journeys don't truly begin until someone takes a first step. So here is a short list of concrete action items to get started:

- Take account of your current financial situation.
- Make a written budget to keep you on track.
- Set specific financial goals.
- Begin paying down your debt.
- Simplify your finances by automating your bills.
- Stop using credit cards.
- Use debit cards to track expenses.
- Set aside an emergency fund.
- Become a frugal spender and avid saver.
- Set aside a percentage of what you earn to give to your church or charity.

2 Earn More by Keeping More

> Suppose one of you wants to build a tower.
> What is the first thing you will do? Won't you
> sit down and figure out how much it will cost
> and if you have enough money to pay for it?
>
> —LUKE 14:28

There's a simple principle of wealth creation that most millionaires instinctively understand. What you don't spend, you get to keep. And the more you decide not to spend, the more you get to keep. That's how you grow a strong and healthy bank account. Wealthy people view money as a road to financial freedom, not as a way to get more stuff. They see it as a means to an end, and the end they're after is far more important to them than a new-smelling car or a flashier wardrobe. That's why the quickest and easiest path to earning more is learning how to keep more. There are thousands of ways to do that; here are some of my favorites.

15 > LEARN HOW AND WHERE TO SHOP

My wife, Ruthie, is a whiz at finding quality, designer clothing and accessories at steep discounts. She knows all the discount shops in our area and always seems to be able to find a bargain. One of the fastest ways to keep more of what you earn is to learn how and where to shop. I'm not suggesting you dumb down your wardrobe by buying cheap clothes, but instead learn how to buy quality, name-brand items at a fraction of the original price. Today there are many discount shops available to those who refuse to pay full retail price. Stores like Stein Mart, Marshalls, Ross, and others offer name-brand clothes and accessories at substantially lower prices for those who have learned how and where to look.

16 > DON'T BE AFRAID TO HAGGLE

Some of my greatest business lessons came from the days of my youth, following my mom around the grocery store as she shopped. With seven mouths to feed, Mom knew better than anyone how to make a dollar stretch. Instead of simply buying fruit and vegetables off the shelf, she'd go to the back of the store and look for the manager of that department—a man she had gotten to know quite well. "What kind of price could I get if I bought a whole box of bananas?" she'd whisper politely. He always gave her a good discount, simply because she was willing to ask. She did the same with sugar, eggs, milk, and clothes. Never underestimate the power of haggling, whether buying from a garage sale or a retail chain store. The best discounts go to those who are willing to ask!

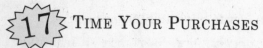 ## 17 TIME YOUR PURCHASES

When you buy can be as important as where you buy. That's why it's a good idea to plan ahead, especially with larger purchases. For instance, if you know you're going to need a new mower soon, wait until the end of summer, when the leaves start to fall. Not only will you find lawn mowers discounted, but the store manager will be eager to deal in order to make room for the new snow blowers. The same principle works for cars. Decide what you want to buy and then wait until the new models start to roll in before walking into the dealership. Salesmen are always more willing to deal when needing to make room for the new inventory. It also helps to wait until the end of the month, since salespeople and managers are working hard to make their quota.

18 BUY USED

Remember all the times you gave perfectly good clothes and household items to Goodwill, simply because your closets were full? Well, everyone does. And because of it, resale stores have racks of perfectly good clothes and household items priced at pennies on the dollar. There are tremendous bargains to be had for those willing to buy used—whether it's vehicles, appliances, clothes, or furniture. Why fork out a big part of your retirement savings for a new car when one with a little experience can bring you the same thrill for far less money? Educate yourself on the best places to shop for used items. Garage sales can be gold mines of bargains, and so can the classified section of your newspaper or Craigslist or even Thrifty Nickel. It's fun, adventurous, and a smart way to save a bundle.

19 THINK "QUALITY," NOT EXPENSIVE

Here's a true story I like to call "The Tale of Two Appliances." Once upon a time (about five years ago) my wife needed a dishwasher, and being the good husband, I bought the most expensive one I could find. It was a top-of-the-line dishwasher with all the bells and whistles, controlled by a computer circuit board built into the door. About this same time, we needed a new clothes dryer, but instead of buying the most expensive one, we decided to buy the sturdiest, least-expensive dryer in the store. Since that time the dryer has worked like a charm. The dishwasher, however, has been repaired three times and right now is completely dead. We're in the market for a new one. The moral to the story is simple. When buying, think "quality," not expensive. Sometimes less really is more.

20 POSTPONE PURCHASES

Whenever possible, try putting off buying items that you need until you know you've found the best deal. Most people decide they need a certain appliance or set of curtains and then spend the day driving from store to store until they find it. But that's not how you locate a bargain. Instead, try holding off and watching for the best deal. Locate the color and brand you want, and then wait for it to go on sale. Ask the store manager how often this particular department posts discounts or when he expects they might have store markdowns. Waiting also gives you time to look around, even shop online, just to make sure you're getting the best possible price. People who are patient and persistent almost always get the best deals.

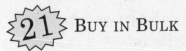 ## 21 BUY IN BULK

This only works if you have space to store things, but household items are always cheaper if you can buy in bulk—especially groceries. Instead of buying just what you need for the coming few days, think ahead and buy items in bulk at a warehouse store, like Sam's Club or Costco. Most canned and bottled foods have long shelf lives, as do many packaged staples, like rice, beans, and sugar. Take time to do the math and see how much you can save by buying in bulk things you regularly use, then make space for them in a closet or cupboard. The same holds true for other household items, like batteries, light bulbs, and toilet paper. But beware! Not all bulk items are priced cheaper, so do your homework before buying.

22 CUT NEEDLESS EXPENSES

Think you can't get by without your morning latte or noon lunch with friends? Think again, because plenty of people do. Especially people on a tight budget. If you need to cut corners, this is the first (sometimes most painful) place to start. You can save a big chunk of cash by simply cutting unnecessary expenses. Instead of paying $4 for a cup of coffee, learn to make it yourself each morning. Try different blends until you learn to get it just right. And while you're at it, target other needless expenses, like movies, manicures, alcohol, cigarettes, and expensive car washes. All of these things can take a huge bite out of a small budget. Small expenses always feel small until you start to add them up at the end of the month.

23 STEER CLEAR OF JUNK FOOD

Some food items simply cost more than others. And as a general rule of thumb, the worse it is for your body, the more expensive it is. Things like chips, sodas, and candy can add a whopping price tag to your grocery bill, while the healthiest foods are usually pretty wallet friendly. Make a list of things you need before you go, and then stick to it. Fill your list with things like fruit, vegetables, milk, meat, cheese, and eggs—things you can use to throw together a quick, healthy meal. Remember to pick up plenty of bagged pastas and canned foods—things that are economical, healthy, and easy to fix. Your wallet will thank you, your budget will thank you, and best of all, your waistline will thank you!

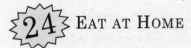 24 Eat at Home

Meals prepared at home are usually less expensive and more nutritious than dining out. You can save both time and money by cooking large portions and saving for future lunches and dinners. Our kids love breakfast burritos, so Ruthie often takes some extra time to make a couple of dozen egg, cheese, and bacon burritos and then wraps them individually for the freezer. In the morning she throws a couple in the microwave for a hearty breakfast for the kids. Preparing ahead also works for lunch and supper. Try making several casseroles and keeping them in the freezer for quick and delicious dinners. And if you feel too rushed in the morning to pack a lunch, do it at night before you go to bed. Anytime you can avoid restaurant food, you'll come out ahead of the game financially.

25 > JOIN A FOOD CO-OP

What's a food co-op? In short, it's a store that's owned by the people who shop there. Unlike most major grocery stores, which are owned by shareholders or private firms, co-ops are owned and operated by their members. This tends to keep the quality high and the prices low. Food co-ops come in all shapes and sizes, but most specialize in local, natural, and organic products. They're also community oriented, offering lots of benefits, from clothing and recipe exchanges to cooking classes. And they tend to be volunteer run, which means you'll probably have to help out from time to time. Not all co-ops are created equal, so do your homework before joining one. But for the discriminating shopper, it's a great chance to buy quality food at a discounted price.

26 > KEEP YOUR CAR SERVICED

If you want to stay away from high monthly car payments, then you need to keep your car running smoothly—and as long as possible. That means keeping it running in top shape. It goes without saying that the oil needs to be changed regularly, but there are other maintenance issues that are just as important. Like checking the fluids, brakes, transmission, and other important moving parts. Take an active role in keeping your car maintained properly, and you'll avoid costly repair bills down the road. Even little things can make a big difference. Keeping tires properly inflated not only helps them last longer but actually helps save gas—as much as three to four miles per gallon in some cases. So take care of one of your largest investments, and it will take care of you.

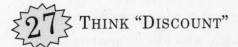 Think "Discount"

I write for a living, which means I do lots of reading and researching. Because of this, I buy more books than the average person (probably far more than I need). I love the convenience of picking up what I need at the local bookstore, but before heading out, I always check the store's Web site to see if any coupons are available online. I also make sure I'm on my favorite store's mailing lists. And I watch for the monthly catalogs and e-mail updates. These almost always come with coupons worth 20 percent or even 30 percent off my next purchase. Almost all stores cater to regular customers by offering discount mailings and e-mails. And there are good bargains on new and used books through on-line outlets, too, if you are willing to pay shipping and handling costs and wait a few days for delivery. Whatever items you use on a regular basis, there are ways to get them at a steep discount. All you have to do is look.

28 THINK "eBAY"

Another great place for bargains is eBay, especially when buying items that aren't electronic. I'm a motorcycle enthusiast, and motorcycle parts can be extremely expensive. If you own one, you know what I mean. Recently I was in the market for a simple leather windshield bag, and the local shops wanted anywhere from $40 to $90 for them. I found a brand-new one on eBay for $14. In fact, I've outfitted my entire bike with items I bought on eBay, from handgrips to saddlebags—even a new windshield—and saved boatloads of money in the process. It takes a little work and research, but if you want a real bargain on the things you need, learn how to use eBay. It's as fun as it is economical.

29 Think "Craigslist"

I could write an entire book on the joys of buying and selling on Craigslist. I wish I'd thought of it, because it's an ingenious idea—and a great way to connect with other buyers and sellers. If you know how to use it, you can save tremendous amounts of money. We recently decided to buy our son a newer car for college—preferably a four-wheel-drive, since we live in Colorado. Since 4x4s don't come cheap in the mountains, we started browsing Craigslist in other parts of the country. We found a great low-mileage SUV for him in Branson, Missouri, easily saving $4,000 in the process. My wife and I flew out to get it, even took a short vacation while we were there, and still came out on top. In fact, we've bought our last four cars online, and each time we saved a bundle.

30 Think "Free"

Okay, this may seem like a stretch, but there are tons of free items out there if you're willing to look. I wouldn't suggest looking for free food or furniture, but what about things like lumber or firewood? As a child, I spent many a weekend helping my dad remove trees and stumps for people who simply wanted them taken away. They were more than willing to pay for our services, and when we got home, we'd cut up the tree limbs and stack them by the house for firewood. Dad was also a weekend carpenter, so he frequented construction sites and got to know the foremen. Often they would have lots of perfectly good wood for anyone willing to haul it off. And this isn't junk wood we're talking about— often it was oak and walnut cabinets left over from a full-kitchen-remodel job. Dad got the wood simply because he was willing to ask.

PUTTING YOUR PLAN INTO ACTION

Frugal living may begin as a desire to get ahead by saving extra money, but your ultimate goal should be to make it a lifestyle choice, not just a short-term solution to your problems. Let's recap what we've learned about keeping more of what we've earned:

- Become a smart shopper.
- Never be afraid to haggle.
- Learn when to buy.
- Consider buying used whenever possible.
- Buy quality items, not expensive ones.
- Put off major purchases when you can.
- Learn to buy in bulk.
- Buy only what you need.
- Eat healthy, home-cooked meals.
- Look into joining a food co-op.
- Keep your car serviced.
- Save by shopping online.
- Get what you can for free.

3 Increase Your Income at Work

Committed and persistent work pays off.
—PROVERBS 28:20

I've been in business for over thirty years and in that time have hired and managed hundreds of people—probably over a thousand if I did the math. I've seen every imaginable type of employee, from lazy and ungrateful to incredibly gifted and productive. I've seen people who wouldn't know a good day's work if it bit them in the you-know-what, and others who worked circles around everyone in their path. I've learned that in the world of business, no two employees are created equal. And when I get good ones, I do whatever it takes to keep them. If you want to increase your income at work, there are numerous ways to do it. But it takes an intentional effort. Here are some simple ways to do just that.

31 ⟩ PROTECT YOUR JOB

Keeping your job intact is a priority in any economy, but it becomes especially important during a national recession. Even bad jobs are hard to come by when the economy starts to nosedive. So if your goal is to increase your family income, step one is to hold on to your job, whatever it takes. Recent news on the economy is not good. Banks are not lending, costs are rising, profits are dwindling, and some of the country's oldest and largest corporations are starting to fold. In the process, unemployment numbers are rising by the hour. Some have said that we're headed toward the worst economy we've seen since the Great Depression. Though I don't share that view, I do believe we're headed for some seriously tough years. So if you have a job, be thankful and hang on to it!

32 ⟩ KNOW WHAT YOU'RE WORTH

Regardless of economic conditions, you need to know that you're being paid a fair wage for the work you do. And that means keeping up with the standard industry rates in your area of expertise. I've seen huge variations in pay between employees doing the same work—even ones who work side by side. And often there's no reason for it, other than one struck a better deal with the employer. You could start asking around to see what your co-workers are making, but that wouldn't make you very popular where you work. Instead, do your research on the Internet. Salary.com is a good place to start. They have a great online tool for gauging what you should be making in your industry and city. The first step in trying to earn more at work is to make sure you're getting what you're worth in the first place.

33 > STAY VISIBLE

Nobody likes a guy who toots his own horn, but when it comes to the workplace, you do have to make your accomplishments known. You don't have to be arrogant about it, but you have to be smart. If you've been responsible for landing large accounts for your firm, you deserve the recognition. It's not important that your co-workers remember, but it is important that your boss understands how valuable you are to the bottom line. Try keeping track of your accomplishments by documenting ways you've either brought in extra business or saved the company money. Make it detailed, along with dates, facts, and figures. Then carry it with you during employee evaluations. It will also come in handy if you ever need to apply for another job or if asking for a raise. Which isn't a bad idea anytime you think you're not getting what you deserve.

34 ASK FOR A RAISE

Obviously, if you see pink slips being passed out at your workplace, it's not a great time to ask for more money. But if you've been an asset to the company and find that you're being underpaid for your work, there's no shame in asking for better compensation. Begin by familiarizing yourself with your company's pay practices. If they tend to give raises during the annual review season, it's unlikely you'll get one during other months, so time your approach. Document your accomplishments, along with any other info that might help, like added responsibilities you've taken on, important achievements, or additional training you've completed. Then make an appointment with your supervisor. Have a specific amount in mind you want to ask for—and be reasonable. If you're worth more, chances are you'll get it. If not, it's time to start making yourself more valuable.

35 MAKE YOURSELF INDISPENSABLE

Every company needs those foundational employees who think ahead—people who understand the challenges of today's business world and are willing to go above and beyond the call of duty to excel in the industry. Companies need problem solvers, not problem shifters. They need forward-thinking people who get along with their bosses and co-workers, who know how to deal well with customers, who fight for the company's interest when dealing with vendors, who aren't afraid to tackle big projects on tight budgets. People who are low-maintenance, high-output, noncomplaining, ever-positive producers. People who aren't afraid to wipe out the microwave before an important meeting. These kinds of people are indispensable, and bosses know it. So if you really want to keep your job and make more than your co-workers, be that person.

36 ASK FOR EXTRA WORK

Almost all companies have work-load overflows from time to time. Often these jobs fall to the supervisors or team managers, and they have to find a way to get them done. They usually give the task to someone they know won't complain—their most dependable worker. If you're not being asked to do these jobs, that's not a great sign. You won't likely be the first name mentioned when raises are being discussed behind closed doors. If you're looking to increase your income, ask your boss if there is any extra work you can do. If it pays extra, that's great. If it doesn't, ask for it anyway. Your obvious work ethic and dedication to the company will come in handy when it comes time to ask for more money.

 ## 37 ⟩ BE A PROBLEM SOLVER

The test of a truly successful person is not the ability to keep problems from happening but the ability to solve them when they do. People make mistakes, and the more people you have interacting together, the more mistakes are likely to happen. Some of those mistakes can be devastating to a company's bottom line. That's why problem solvers are so critical to a firm's survival in the marketplace. When you get right down to it, the difference between a thriving company and a faltering one is simply the ability to fix mistakes when they happen and move past them. Learn to be the first person on the scene when a breakdown happens and the first one to come up with a solution, and you're almost guaranteed a spot on your boss's list when bonuses and salary increases are being passed around.

38 VERBALIZE YOUR AMBITION

I'm always amazed at how few people in the workplace actually verbalize their career goals. Right now I have a number of people on staff, yet only a handful have told me about their aspirations within the company. I know that one man is working hard to become a manager, and he'll be there as soon as our work load can support it. He's reminded me on a number of occasions about this goal, just to make sure I don't forget. I have other employees who are excellent at what they do, yet they have never shown any desire to advance. I usually assume that they're happy where they are. Even if they're not, chances are slim that I'll promote them further, simply because they haven't shown the ambition I need to see in order to trust them with greater responsibility. If you really want to get ahead at work, make sure your boss knows it.

 39 DRESS FOR SUCCESS

I could write an entire book on this subject. Oh wait…someone already has. And it's a great read, by the way. *Dress for Success* was written by John T. Molloy and published by Grand Central Publishing. Though it was first written in the seventies, it's been updated several times and is still pertinent to today's fashions. If you haven't read it, you should definitely take the time, because it's filled with excellent advice on the virtues of looking successful in order to become successful. In the book, Molloy explains how talent, savvy, and dress all work together to create a winning employee and how all are critical to moving ahead in the workplace. You don't want to outshine your clients or bosses, but you do want to look like you belong in the same league. And that's a huge step in the right direction when trying to increase your income.

40 WORK AT HOME

For those who have the discipline and ambition, working at home is a good way to increase your income. Not only does it save on transportation expenses, but it can save big chunks of time and can often help you be more productive, since workplaces tend to be breeding grounds for wasted time. If you have a job that allows you the option of working at home, even on a part-time basis, ask if you can try it out. Then use the opportunity to be as productive as possible. It may be tempting to slack off and play, but resist the urge. Remember, the point is to show that you have the company's best interest at heart and that you can be trusted to produce, even when no one is there to watch over you. Give it a try and see if it doesn't get the attention of your superiors!

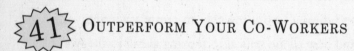

41 OUTPERFORM YOUR CO-WORKERS

This may seem like a no-brainer, but in the real world of commerce it's unusual to see someone actually trying to be better and faster than those they work with. There's an interesting dynamic that tends to happen in most offices. People usually match the pace being set by others. When one person takes a break, others usually drop what they're doing and go on break as well. When the clock strikes 5 p.m. and the first employee starts to leave, others instinctively follow. The herd mentality is staggeringly predictable. But what happens when one person breaks away from the pack?

When she rises above the herd and starts to outshine the others? Trust me, the bosses take notice. So instead of following the work pace of others, be the one in your office to set the standard.

 ## STRENGTHEN YOUR PEOPLE SKILLS

People with exceptional interpersonal skills always tend to rise to the top—in their careers, their businesses, and life in general. We've all seen it. Take any two people with the same skill sets, the same opportunities, even the same basic looks, and the one who knows how to communicate and get along well with others will inevitably be the one who gets ahead. And these kinds of skills can easily be learned, even if you weren't born with them. No other skill set is as critical to advancement as excellent people skills. Those who have them can better communicate ideas; win others to their way of thinking; build immediate rapport with customers, co-workers, and superiors; deal with conflict and confrontation; and basically create a more pleasant workplace atmosphere. If you haven't worked at developing your people skills, you're already behind the power curve, so make it a priority, starting today.

{43} Be Prompt and Courteous

You'd be surprised how many people show up late to meetings and basically forget to be courteous to others in the workplace. Think about what it says to your boss when you show up just one minute late for a meeting. You might as well stamp "unreliable" on your forehead. And if you're unreliable, so are your ideas, your projects, even your personal character. That's not a good message to send if you're looking to advance in the company. Make a habit of being five minutes early for every appointment—even if you have to wait on the other person. Do this whether you're meeting with a customer, your supervisor, or a co-worker. Act as if every meeting you attend is the most important meeting of your career, because you never know when that might just be the case.

{44} Be Relevant

There's an old saying in the world of business: "If you want something done, give it to a busy person." If you've found yourself busy at work, be thankful, because that means you've made yourself relevant. If you're the person who others look for when they have a question about the new computers, or which forms to use for a purchase request, or where the staples are kept, then congratulations! You've made yourself relevant. If your boss depends on you to stay abreast of new technologies and explain to the team how to work the new digital-conferencing projector, then you're likely to be first in line for a pay increase, because—you guessed it—you are relevant. But if you're the one depending on a co-worker for those kinds of things, then you've got some work to do. Make yourself relevant and your employer will notice.

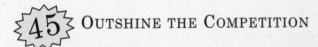 **OUTSHINE THE COMPETITION**

There's one strategy for getting ahead in the workplace and raising your earning potential that overshadows all others. And that is to consciously and proactively help your company outshine the competition. Nothing will help you get ahead faster. There are numerous ways to do that, but here are three simple ones worth remembering. First, keep your eye on the company's bottom line. Cut expenses where you can, and grow revenues at every opportunity—even if that's not your job. Second, actively look for ways to make your

company more competitive in the marketplace. If you identify a problem that's holding your company back, find a way
to fix it. Third, provide exceptional customer service and see
that everyone you work with does the same thing. When
your company profits, you have a good chance of profiting
along with it!

PUTTING YOUR PLAN INTO ACTION

Any employee who learns to stand out from the crowd will inevitably be in the driver's seat when it comes to succeeding in the workplace. Let's go over a few basic rules to help you do just that:

- Do what it takes to keep your job.
- Research your worth in the job market.
- Make your accomplishments known.
- Ask for a raise at the right time and place.
- Make yourself valuable.
- Look for extra work.
- Be a problem solver, not a problem causer.
- Let your aspirations be known.
- Dress for the job you want, not the one you have.
- Work at home when you can.
- Outperform others in the workplace.
- Increase your knowledge and skills.
- Be on time; be relevant.
- Make your company's interest your primary interest.

4 Simple Ways to Earn Extra Cash

He who gathers money little
by little makes it grow.
—PROVERBS 13:11

Maximizing your earning potential at work is always a good idea, regardless of the current economic condition. But there are times when what you need most is a little extra cash. Maybe you need money for a new car or to put a child through college or to pay off some unexpected bills. It may be a short-term problem or a need to supplement your income for the long haul. Whatever your need, there are countless ways to bring in extra money for your family. Most of these ideas can be done on a part-time basis, during weekend hours, or a few evenings a week—or perhaps by a stay-at-home parent. This isn't an exhaustive list, but it's a good place to begin if your wallet is in need of a little jump-start!

46 START AN eBAY BUSINESS

I love eBay! I've been buying and selling on eBay for years, and I can't think of a better way to earn extra cash in a short amount of time. The learning curve for sellers is much shorter than you might expect. The site is already set up with all the tools and advice you need to have your eBay business up and running in one productive afternoon. The best place to begin is to simply visit the site and start going through the tutorials. They provide detailed advice on everything from setting up your site to deciding what you should sell. They say that every eBay success story is a tale of trial and error, so don't expect to figure it all out the first day. But once you find your niche, you'll wonder why it took you so long to get on board.

47 USE CRAIGSLIST

Craigslist is another great tool for raising cash by selling items you don't need—especially larger items that might be too expensive to ship. But don't just decide to sell something and then get online to list it. Do some preparatory work.

Begin by making the item presentable. If you're selling a used couch, rent a machine and clean it first. A little effort can make all the difference in the price you can get. Then research similar items already listed on Craigslist to find out the going rate. Once you have a fair price, take good photos. Items listed without pictures or with poorly lit pictures get a fraction of the attention. Post closeup pictures of any flaws or dings, just to let buyers know you're honest. Then describe the item in detail in the listing. Take time to do it right, and you'll get top dollar for everything you sell.

48 ⟩ BUY AND SELL "JUNK"

We've had a number of garage sales through the years, and each time we do I notice an interesting dynamic. As soon as we start setting up for the sale, people are waiting for us in the driveway. They never ask if they can start shopping early, they just start going through our stuff. And they always seem to be on a mission. Some will be looking only for glass items, while others ask if we have any tools. Some look only at clothes— and buy anything that looks nice, regardless of the size. Many of these people are junk dealers, looking for things they can sell and consign. And they know instinctively what will bring them a profit. If you have the time, buying and selling other people's junk is a great way to bring in extra cash.

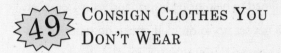

CONSIGN CLOTHES YOU DON'T WEAR

Almost all of us buy more clothes than we need. We find something on sale or buy a new shirt on impulse, then when we get home we find that it doesn't fit the way we thought or the colors don't quite appeal to us. We seldom take time to return these items, especially if we bought them at a discount. So they hang in our closet, taking up space and cluttering our lives even more. Eventually we get the bug to de-clutter, so we pull them out and pack them in a box for Goodwill. I like giving to charity, but if you're short on cash, why not take time to consign those clothes instead? There are consignment stores all over the country just begging for items to sell, and they know how to price and display items to get top price.

 ## SELL UNWANTED BOOKS AND DVDS

We all buy books and movies that interest us, but once we've read or watched them, there's no reason to keep them around anymore. Unless you use books for research, like I do, why not sell them for some extra cash? The absolute best way to do that is to list them on Amazon.com. Just like eBay, Amazon is designed to help bring buyers and sellers together, and it's easy to get set up to do it. If you're not already registered on Amazon as a buyer, you'll have to do that first. Then click on the link that says "Sell Your Stuff," and you're ready to list. In many ways it's much easier than eBay and can be just as profitable. Both books and DVDs sell well on Amazon, and you have a worldwide customer base.

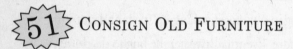 ## 51 CONSIGN OLD FURNITURE

Consigning antiques and furniture is a bit more complicated than consigning clothes, but the basic rules remain the same. You need to get items in the best possible shape before taking them in for an appraisal. This means cleaning the pieces well, maybe even touching up the stain or paint (or repainting altogether). You also need to replace any lost hinges or handles and tighten all the screws. Furniture consigners expect things to be in top condition before putting them on their floor. There are exceptions to this, like when you have an antique piece that shows a lot of "character flaws." But even then it needs to be cleaned and treated with wood conditioner first. If you know the history of the piece, share it with the consignor. This is valuable information when trying to sell antiques. A good dealer can get you top dollar for that furniture cluttering your garage.

52 ⟩ Take a Second Job

In my business I use lots of part-time help. In fact, I'd rather hire people for a few hours in the evening than take on a full-time employee. Often part-timers are more productive, simply because they work only a few hours a day. And they don't depend on me as their primary source of income, making it easy to develop a real friendship with them, instead of a boss/employee relationship—which has a different dynamic. If you're in need of extra cash, taking on a part-time job is a great solution. But if you do, don't look at it as a long-term arrangement. Determine going in what you plan to use the money for, and then don't allow yourself to start adding new monthly bills. That will completely defeat the purpose. Your goal is to raise extra cash, not to dig deeper into debt.

53 ⟩ Provide Household Services

Every year around Thanksgiving time, we start seeing signs crop up in the neighborhood. They say things like Will Decorate Your House for Christmas or No Time to Shop? Let Us Help. These signs are put up by industrious people who understand their market. Most upper-middle-class people are willing to pay others to do things they don't have time to do. And wealthy people are willing to pay for just about everything they need done, from running errands to taking the dogs for a walk each evening. These tasks don't take much skill, just time and a willingness to do them. If you're looking for some part-time cash, try making some signs of your own. Better yet, run ads in your local newspaper. Once you get your first job, ask them to tell all their friends you're available. Word of mouth is the best advertising.

54 ⟩ Take a Seasonal Job

If you're not the primary breadwinner in your house, and all you need is some extra cash—without the burden of a long-time career—think about taking a seasonal job. There are many industries that need help for a short time during the

year, and they look for people who don't want a year-round
commitment. Christmas is the most obvious time to look,
since stores often need extra help for the holiday rush. But
there are other opportunities far more exciting. Like working on a cruise ship. There are many entry-level jobs available, from deck hands to maids to gift-shop clerks. It's a great
way to make extra cash while seeing the world! Ski resorts
also need seasonal help, from instructors to front-desk workers in the resort. And some resorts even offer free ski passes
to the help.

55 ⟩ TEACH PART-TIME

You don't necessarily need a teaching degree to teach part-
time. Many private schools and charter schools are not
bound by the same rules as public schools, so they're more
interested in your ability to teach than what degree you have.
You'll likely have to have some sort of college degree first,
but it doesn't have to be in education. If you know how to
control a classroom and can work your way through a text-
book with the class, then consider being a substitute teacher.
Also, many community colleges and universities are looking
for part-time professors to teach evening classes. If you have

at least a master's degree in your field and a level of expertise in your career, then you're the exact person they're looking for. It's a great part-time job for someone who isn't afraid to stand in front of a crowd.

56 } BECOME A CONSULTANT

Everyone is an expert at something. What you do at work may seem second nature to you, but to others, your knowledge is valuable information. Maybe you've had to master a specific type of software or maintain complicated telephone systems at work. Maybe you've built a successful career selling cars. Whatever your expertise, someone is likely willing to pay for your advice. There's no hidden secret to becoming a consultant. You simply need to organize your thoughts and then let people know you're available. Start by printing up a small brochure listing your level of expertise, years in business, accomplishments, and availability. Research fair rates on the Internet, then set your price. Start by targeting small businesses that are more likely to need help with your skill sets. Once you get started, build your reputation through referrals. It's not rocket science (though if that's your expertise, be sure to set your rates high!).

57 ⬡ EARN FROM YOUR HOBBIES

One woman named Laura loved building dollhouses as a child. And as she grew, the dollhouses she built became more intricate and elaborate. Soon others began asking her if she would consider selling them, so she did. And the more she sold, the more people wanted them. Laura had become an expert at her hobby, and before she knew it, she had the funds to open a small dollhouse shop. Her part-time hobby developed into a full-time, thriving business. You may not want to grow your hobby into a career, but you can certainly turn it into some part-time cash. Instead of simply spending money on your hobby, think of ways you can buy and sell in order to profit from it. There are Web sites that might even hire you as a guest contributor on the topic. Do your research, get creative, and see what happens.

58 ⬡ SELL STOCK PHOTOS

The age of digital photography has opened up a wealth of opportunity for those with an eye for framing and taking good pictures. Equipment is cheaper than ever, making it easy for even weekend shutterbugs to take exceptional photos.

And there are places online set up to help you sell them. Magazines, graphic artists, and online webzines are always searching these sites for royalty-free, promotional photos. I've been co-publishing a fly-fishing magazine for several years, and we often buy stock photos for advertisements or filler shots. Your best bet when selling photos online is to develop a niche. Think about the kind of photography you're best at, like sports, people, or landscapes. Specializing will help you hone your skills and also narrow your market when looking for a place to list them. An afternoon of online research should get you started.

59 BLOG FOR PAY

If you have a field of expertise and can write clearly, there is money to be made in online blogging. I've actually been a bit skeptical of this idea since blogging for pay is a relatively new concept, but I have several friends who have proven me wrong. One is a major history buff who has a brain full of seemingly useless historical facts and figures. He discovered an online site willing to pay him to post relevant and interesting historical articles and then interact with people who read his columns and post questions. He has a blast writing his blogs and actually gets paid for it. Another is an IT specialist who gets paid to write reviews of new high-tech gadgets as they come on to the market. If you have something to say, see if someone is willing to pay you for it.

60 › TAKE IN A BOARDER

You could always move into a cardboard box and rent your house out for extra cash, but if that's not an option, why not consider renting out a spare room? If your kids have flown the nest, this is a great opportunity to make back some of the money they cost you through the years. This works especially well if you live near a college or university. Students are always looking for a place to rent that won't cost an arm and a leg. You need to make sure your house is set up for it, since you don't want to be sharing a bathroom. You also need to screen the applicants extremely well. The best approach is to find someone referred by a friend or family member—or maybe a local campus minister. Keep your price reasonable, and you're sure to find the perfect boarder.

61   PART-TIME MODELING

Okay, so you don't have capped teeth and six-pack abs. That doesn't mean you can't make money as a supermodel! Or at least an average model. Plenty of regular-looking people make money modeling part-time for ad agencies or magazines. My kids have several teenage friends who have made extra cash modeling for hair salons or local clothing stores. Any time a company is hired to put together a catalog, they're in need of fresh-looking, attractive people to smile for the camera and look happy. Cute kids are especially in demand, and what kid isn't cute? Try watching the paper for casting calls, or send e-mails and photos to local ad agencies letting them know of your availability. You may just be the exact fresh face they're looking for. You won't know unless you try.

PUTTING YOUR PLAN INTO ACTION

There are endless ways to generate extra cash. The key is to think outside the box and be creative. You'll be surprised at all the ideas you might come up with. But for now, let's recap the ideas we've discussed:

- Sell items through eBay or Craigslist.
- Learn to buy and sell other people's "junk."
- Make money by cleaning out your closets.
- Sell books and DVDs you don't need.
- Sell furniture cluttering up your garage.
- Take on a part-time job.
- Provide services for others.
- Consider a seasonal job.
- Become a part-time teacher or consultant.
- Make money with your hobbies.
- Sell photos online.
- Become an online blogger.
- Rent out a room.
- Become a catalog model.

5 Home-Based Businesses

Work your garden—you'll end up with plenty of food;
play and party—you'll end up with an empty plate.

—PROVERBS 28:19

When most people think of going into business, they imagine renting a storefront property and filling it with inventory, selling antiques and collectibles, repairing computers, or another retail-type venture. But I've always been partial to home-based businesses. I like businesses with low overhead, minimum start-up costs, and a well-defined customer base. I like the freedom of seeking out your customers instead of opening up a shop and hoping they find you. It takes more discipline to be home based, but the long-term rewards are worth the added effort.

There are countless home-based businesses worth looking into, but here's a short list of my personal favorites.

62 CHILD CARE IN YOUR HOME

The demand for high-quality day-care services has never been greater. Parents are constantly seeking a warm, caring, friendly environment for their kids while they're at work, and people who can provide that for them will always have plenty of business. Day care has become one of the fastest-growing segments of the home-business economy over the last few years. And the trend doesn't seem to be slowing. Statistics show that it's not uncommon for a home day-care business to net over $50,000 a year in profits—even more if you're ambitious and willing to expand. Each state and city has different rules regarding home day care, so do your research before jumping in. But if you like kids and know how to run a tight ship, this could be your ticket to self-employment.

63 PROFESSIONAL TUTORING

Many people enjoy teaching kids but don't want the hassle of working for the school system. They don't want to be tied up five days a week with a classroom full of kids. Becoming a professional tutor is a good option. It takes a little work to build up your client base, but the hours are flexible, the pay per hour tends to be better, and you often just have one child at a time to teach. It can also be incredibly rewarding. Parents and schools are always on the lookout for someone willing to tutor kids on an independent basis. Start by contacting private, charter, and public schools in your area to let them know you're available. Get a résumé to them that includes any specialized credentials or teaching degrees you might have. You can also advertise in the paper or on school bulletin boards.

64 CATERING

We have a friend who can cook and entertain like a pro. She has a knack for putting together four-course meals fit for a king and knows how to set an elegant table with fine china and silverware. She also knows how to throw an impromptu barbecue, with four kinds of meat and all the fixings, served in elegant, casual style. No matter what she does, it always turns out great. We've encouraged her many times to start her own catering business because she'd be a huge success.

For those with a flair for cooking and throwing a party, catering can be a great business—either part- or full-time. Like many home businesses, this one would depend on lots of referrals, but if you've gained a reputation as a good cook, this should be an easy hurdle. Just have some cards printed and let your friends know you're in business.

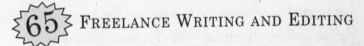 ## 65 FREELANCE WRITING AND EDITING

Here's a business I know something about. I've been making a good part-time income writing and editing for over sixteen years, and it never gets old. Writing is a passion of mine, and I know how to deliver a decent manuscript on time, so the work just tends to follow me around. Like most writers, I started my career wanting to be an author and was lucky enough to get several books published. Since that time I've stayed busy as a ghostwriter and collaborator for numerous preachers and celebrities. I've written hundreds of articles on dozens of different topics, and I also write family commentaries for nonprofit organizations. It can get intense, but it never gets boring. If you have a way with words and something to say, consider freelance writing or editing.

66 WEB DESIGN AND MAINTENANCE

I'm convinced that English is my son's second language—right behind computer code. Even as a kid he was more comfortable working a mouse than a dinner fork. And a lot of his friends are the same way. Because of this gift, my son has been making money designing and maintaining Web sites since he was fourteen—only because he did it for free before then. He's designed sites that impress even the most seasoned designers. David's now in college getting degrees in graphic design and marketing. I'm certain he'll always make a good living at this, but the truth is, you don't have to have his level of talent to be a successful Web designer. With today's user-friendly software, almost anyone can create a decent Web presence. And if you learn to do it well, you have a great business opportunity at your fingertips.

67 PET GROOMING

We have a dog, but that's all he is. He's our dog. He's part of the family, of course, and we love him dearly, but he's still just an everyday, garden-variety house pet. So we don't spend a lot of money keeping him groomed and combed and walked properly—which is why he's lazier than Aunt Verna's left eye. But we know that we're in the vast minority on this. We know people who spend more on their pets than on their kid's college education—which is why pet-grooming businesses are booming. You don't have to have any special skills, just a willingness to learn how. There are six-week courses that can teach you all you need to have a thriving business and even give you a diploma to hang on your wall—just in case you run across a snooty poodle who can read!

68 PET TRAINING

This is another great business that caters to pet lovers. Who doesn't want a well-trained dog? One that comes when you call him, stays when you tell him to, and knows where he can and can't make messes? Pet trainers have to learn their craft before hanging out a shingle, but it's something anyone can do with the right patience and level of desire. I'm guessing you need to really like animals to do this. And you can't be overly obsessed about poop or dog germs or other career hazards. But if you're good with animals and think you have what it takes, pet training can be a great business. There are online schools that offer full training and certification for under $3,000 (probably cheaper if you take time to look), so it's a career that's more affordable than many others to get into—on a part- or full-time basis.

69 HOME INSPECTION AND APPRAISAL SERVICE

My dad would have made a great home inspector in his day. He loved tinkering around the house, building things, fixing things, or simply figuring out how things worked in case he ever needed to fix them. He was a handyman's handyman. If that describes you, then why not look into a home inspection and appraisal business? It's the perfect line of work for someone with a basic understanding of home construction and repair. A background as a builder would make you particularly qualified, but that's not crucial. Mostly you need a desire to learn and a penchant for crawling into tight spaces. You have to get qualified first, and that may mean going to school to learn. Check with your local home-builders association and they can steer you in the right direction to get started.

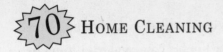 70 Home Cleaning

I'm not sure there is a faster, easier way to bring in extra money than starting a home-cleaning business. You probably have everything you need to get started right in your closet, and getting clients is often as easy as putting the word out among your friends. With so many families depending on two incomes, people are always in search of a good, honest housecleaner. And you don't have to be Mary Poppins to do it. You just have to have basic cleaning skills. People who clean houses readily attest to the satisfaction they get from leaving a room looking and smelling great. And cleaning isn't drudgery when you're paid well to do it. You can build the business as large as you want or choose to keep it small and personal. Either way, you'll have flexible hours and good money.

71 Handyman Service

I have a friend who spent years as a general contractor. In that time he built and sold dozens of high-end custom homes. He was good at what he did, but his life was filled with frustration. He was constantly dealing with incompetent subcontractors, rising lumber costs, and hard-to-please customers. So a few years ago he decided to use his skills and start a handyman service. He said it was the best decision he's ever made. At first he did most of the work himself, but it wasn't long before he had to bring on extra help. Today he has a booming handyman business with a few dozen full- and part-time workers. If you're handy with tools, this may be the perfect business for you. Just make sure you have the proper licenses before jumping in.

72 ⟩ REAL-ESTATE MANAGEMENT

There's one upside to a down economy. If you've maintained a good credit rating and have a little cash on hand, there are many bargains to be had in the real-estate market. In a recession, foreclosures tend to rise by the day, and that drives housing prices down—even in the most expensive parts of the country. This is sad for those losing their homes but a golden opportunity for wise investors. Buying homes and renting them to families in need is a great business if you have the time and wherewithal to do it. Often banks are willing to deal, since they need to get these foreclosed homes off their books. So you're in a position to get a great interest rate. Do your homework before jumping in. Real-estate management can be a tricky business—but highly profitable for the industrious entrepreneur.

73 BUYING AND SELLING REAL ESTATE

My first real job came at the age of fourteen, working for a man who bought and sold houses. His name was John, and he cursed like a drunken sailor, but he knew how to turn a buck. John had gotten to know several good real-estate agents in town and also knew every bank manager by name. Back then foreclosures were rare, but bargains were still to be found. Many of the houses he bought had been condemned by the city because of foundation problems, so he often bought them for pennies on the dollar. Then we'd do whatever it took to repair and rebuild them and get them back on the market. John made a good living flipping houses, and he had learned well how to do it. This is still a great business for those who have the time and knowledge to do it.

74 INTERIOR DESIGN

Even in a struggling economy, interior designers have plenty of work, simply because people tend to hang on to their houses and remodel instead of trading up. Plus, recessions tend to hurt the lower- to middle-class crowd the hardest. People with money always seem to have money, no matter how bad things get. If you have a flair for putting colors and patterns together and love decorating, you probably already have the skills you need. Especially if people are always commenting on how put together your house looks. It takes very little capital to start an interior design business, just a desire to do it and a few good connections. You don't have to have a license in most states, but it wouldn't hurt, so start by looking into what it takes to get accredited. This is another great home business that can be started on a shoestring.

75 BOOKKEEPING

With today's complicated tax structure and government regulations on everything from coal plants to plastic toys (don't get me started!), good bookkeepers will always have plenty to keep them busy. Even the smallest businesses can get buried in paperwork if they don't have someone watching their back. You don't have to have an accounting degree, but you do need basic credentials, which can usually be acquired through a couple years of night classes. Once accredited, many bookkeepers find all the work they want by subcontracting with local accounting firms or outsourcing their services to small- to medium-sized businesses. Tax accountants are especially in demand, though it can be pretty grueling from January through April. In a free-market system, there will always be a need for bean counters, making this a perfect home business for the detail-oriented entrepreneur.

PUTTING YOUR PLAN INTO ACTION

There's a wealth of opportunity in the marketplace for someone with the ambition and wherewithal to start a home-based business. And the type of business you start isn't as important as your commitment to succeed. Let's take a few minutes to recap the short list of ideas we've discussed:

- Provide home day-care service.
- Tutor children.
- Start a catering service.
- Write and edit for pay.
- Become a Web designer.
- Groom or train pets.
- Inspect and appraise homes.
- Start a professional cleaning service.
- Become a professional handyman.
- Manage rental properties.
- Flip houses for profit.
- Do interior decorating.
- Keep books for others.

6 Managing Your Expenses

In the house of the wise are stores of choice food
and oil, but a foolish man devours all he has.

—PROVERBS 21:20

No matter how proficient you become at earning more money and controlling discretionary spending, there are some expenses we all inevitably have to pay. These are the basic costs of getting by, such as housing, utilities, taxes, insurance, and other necessities of life. At times these expenses can feel overwhelming—and out of our control—but they don't have to be. There's a lot you can do to keep your monthly bills from getting the best of you. And it begins by a simple willingness to be diligent, proactive, and vocal. Your creditors have no upside to keeping your expenses low, so that job falls to you. Here are a few concrete things you can do to reduce your monthly outflow of cash.

76 CONSIDER REFINANCING

A lot of factors need to be taken into consideration before deciding to refinance your home. For instance, how long do you plan to be in your home, how much lower will the interest rate be, what are the closing costs for the new loan, what is your equity position in the home, and do you plan to do a cash-out refinancing? It's not as simple as deciding to take advantage of a lower interest rate. As a rule of thumb, if you plan to be in the house a long time and the lower rates seem significant, then meet with a loan expert you trust and look into your options. It's a great idea in some circumstances and a really bad idea in others, so do your homework and use your common sense before pulling the trigger.

77 LOWER YOUR CREDIT CARD INTEREST RATE

Here's the secret to lowering the interest rate on your credit cards: call and ask for a lower rate! That's often all you have to do. It may sound too simple, but savvy people do it every day. I recently financed a business venture using a credit card with a 0 percent interest rate. Cards often offer 0 percent interest for the first six or twelve months in order to gain new customers. At the end of the introductory time the rate kicked in at 10.5 percent, so I called the company and told them I needed a lower rate. They lowered it to 5 percent—which is better than I could get on a business loan. You have to have great credit for this to work, but if you do, there's no quicker way to save hundreds—even thousands of dollars with a simple phone call.

78 Lower Your Home Insurance

If you want to get a truly good deal on home insurance, start by comparing rates online. It's a simple way to keep your company in line, since insurance companies often add unnecessary coverage to your policy in order to charge more. Decide what coverage you really need to feel protected, and only buy that coverage. You can also ask for a higher deductible, like $750 or $1,000, and be prepared to pay that amount if something happens. This one step can often save you a couple of hundred a year in premiums. Also, make sure you get discounts for security items you have, like fire extinguishers, deadbolts, and security alarms. If you don't have these things already, then get them; the insurance savings will more than pay for them. It's not hard to reduce your rate by 10 percent to 20 percent a year, just with a little legwork.

79 LOWER YOUR CAR INSURANCE

Here's where you can see some serious savings with a little effort. Car insurance prices vary pretty wildly from company to company, so be sure you shop around. The Internet is a great place to get rate comparisons. If you can, buy your car and house insurance from the same company since that gives you an automatic 10 to 20 percent discount. You should also raise your deductible to the highest allowable amount. Just increasing it from $200 to $500 can reduce your premiums up to 30 percent, and a $1,000 deductible can save over 40 percent. Some companies offer low-mileage discounts, so if you carpool to work or drive less than 12,000 miles a year, ask your agent about it. There are other discounts offered, but companies won't usually mention them unless you ask, so don't be shy.

$\left\{80\right\}$ Lower Your Health Insurance

The surest and quickest way to lower your health insurance premiums is to simply stay healthy. If you're buying a private-market plan, your premiums are based on your health, and companies consider things like weight, cholesterol, blood pressure, and other health conditions. If you smoke, your rates will be much higher—so quit smoking. You can also ask about a higher deductible, like $1,000 or more. Just make sure you're prepared for the additional expense if something happens. If you need to drastically reduce your rate, consider a catastrophic plan instead of copay-type plan. This means that you'll be covered if you have any major illnesses or accidents, but most of your doctor visits and prescription drugs will have to be paid out of pocket. Find a good agent and inform yourself before buying, and you should be able to save a bundle.

$\left\{81\right\}$ Lower Your Life Insurance

I'm a strong believer in life insurance, especially if you have a young family and you're the primary breadwinner in the home. Life insurance is one of those necessary evils that we all need, just in case something happens. Though a lot of agents argue about the virtues of a whole-life policy, I've never seen one I liked—and I've seen lots of them. I'm still convinced that a low-premium, high-payout term life insurance is the best alternative for most people. Even a forty-year-old man can get a $500,000 term life insurance policy for around $50 a month, and that's not much to spend for the security you're buying. Once again, if you smoke, you'll be paying higher premiums, so quit. Try reapplying thirteen months after quitting and see if you're eligible for better rates.

82 CHECK YOUR CELL PHONE BILLS

I feel like I'm in a never-ending battle with my cell phone provider. And you should be, too, if you're the one paying the bill. I'm constantly amazed at how many strange and ambiguous charges just seem to show up on the monthly statements—things I've never ordered or asked for. I won't mention the name of my provider, but I'm not sure it matters, because I'm convinced they all overcharge in one way or another, and it's your job to keep them honest. Begin by going over the bill closely each time you get it. Make sure you recognize the majority of the phone numbers in your call-activity list. Then check the itemized charges. If you don't understand the statement, call and have them go over it item by item until you do. Don't pay for services you don't use, like Internet access or picture mail.

83 ELIMINATE YOUR LAND LINE

More and more people are doing away with land lines and using cell phones exclusively, and this isn't a bad idea to consider. Especially if you're gone most of the day or work outside the home. Home telephone lines are convenient to have, but they are a lot of added expense if you don't need them. If you have a fax line, it can easily be rerouted through your desktop computer. You'll just have to check into any additional software or hardware you might need to set it up. If you run a business out of your home (as I do) and spend a lot of hours on the phone (again, as I do), then I think having a land line makes sense. But for the average household, this is one area where you could save significant cash over the long haul.

84 Make Payments on Time

Being late on payments is not only unethical, it's extremely costly. And it puts your creditors completely in the driver's seat—which is the last place you want them to be. First of all, late payments tend to carry exorbitant fees—as much as $35 for an average loan or credit card. Plus, when you signed the credit card application, you agreed to allow them to raise the rate if you're ever late. And they will do so without batting an eye. I've seen rates jump to as high as 22 percent as a result of one late payment. Being late also affects your credit rating, which is the single most valuable asset you have. A good credit rating is your greatest tool when trying to keep expenses low. So protect it with a vengeance.

85 Say No to Pushy Cashiers

We've all stood at the store counter as the cashier said, "Would you like to save 10 percent on your purchase by opening up a store charge card?" You say no thank you, but they persist. "You can cancel it at any time, but you'll still get the 10 percent savings on today's purchase. It will just take a minute!" There's a reason these pushy cashiers are so pushy.

Because they get a commission for every application they turn in. And you'd be surprised how many people actually do it. The idea of saving $10 or $20 simply by filling out a form might seem tempting, but don't be taken in. Even if you never plan to use it, the more credit cards you have, the lower your credit rating will be. And remember, your credit rating is your most important asset.

86 KEEP CAREFUL TAX RECORDS

When you're self-employed or have a part-time business venture, good records can save you many dollars at tax time. And good records begin by understanding what kind of records and receipts you need to keep. If you use your car for business purposes, the mileage you drive for work is deductible. If you use it a lot, you might even be able to depreciate that car—or at least a percentage of it. You can also write off any repairs and maintenance to the vehicle—again, at the same percentage rate. There are lots of other deductions available to people, but you have to know about them. I'm convinced that most people actually overpay their taxes, simply because they don't stay informed. So keep good records and find a good tax accountant. This can add up to big savings at the end of the year.

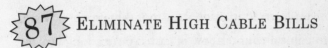 Eliminate High Cable Bills

Does anyone really need premium cable channels piped into their home? Especially people who have little kids in the house? I'm sure it's exciting to have HBO or Showtime or other pay-TV channels at your fingertips (I wouldn't know, because we've never had them), but is it really a necessary expense? More than that, is it really a good use of time and resources? If you don't mind my saying so, I think most of what plays on these channels is trash! For that matter, most network television is inappropriate as well, but at least there are still FCC guidelines at work, keeping some semblance of propriety. The truth is premium cable is expensive, and it's one of the first things you should consider cutting from your budget—even if you aren't struggling financially.

Putting Your Plan into Action

Once you learn to manage your monthly expenses wisely and to control your outflow of cash, you're a long way toward becoming financially independent. These expenses can wreak havoc on even the largest income if you aren't careful. So here again are some key points to remember when taking charge of your bills:

- Look into refinancing your home.
- Keep your interest rates low.
- Keep your insurance premiums low, including home, car, health, and life.
- Don't be overcharged for your cell phone.
- Consider eliminating your home phone service.
- Make all your payments on time.
- Don't be talked into applying for store credit cards.
- Keep good tax records.
- Cancel TV channels you don't need.

7 Saving and Investing Wisely

The one who blesses others is abundantly
blessed; those who help others are helped.

—PROVERBS 11:25

Several years ago our family happened to be in Louisville, Kentucky, during the week of the Kentucky Derby. We were in a restaurant close to the stadium when the race happened, and people went nuts cheering on their favorite horse. In the blink of an eye, it was over and a winner had been crowned. I can see why they call it "the most exciting two minutes in sports." It was the most fast and furious thing I'd ever witnessed—until I decided to try my hand at day-trading stocks. It was a monumental waste of time—and money. When it comes to investing wisely, you need a long-range plan and people who can guide you into the right areas. Here are a few thoughts on getting started.

88 Set Investment Goals

Most people spend more time planning a family vacation than they do planning for retirement. We all dream of what we'd like our life to look like ten, twenty, or even fifty years in the future. But how are we ever going to get there unless we have a specific plan in place? Investment goals are simply written road maps, showing you how to get where you want to be. They include specific amounts you need to save and a time line for saving it. This is where a good financial planner comes in handy. Don't go to a stockbroker or an insurance salesman. They'll usually be more interested in their own investment goals, and that means making a commission off of you! I actually think a Dave Ramsey seminar is the best place to start. His advice is solid and conservative—and he won't steer you wrong.

89 Beware of Stocks

Don't get me wrong, stocks can be a great investment. I've made lots of money investing in stocks. I've also lost lots of money investing in stocks. Anyone invested in the market right now (2009) has likely lost money, since the market has spiraled down. But that doesn't necessarily make them bad investments. It simply highlights the fact that they are riddled with risk. The stock market was never intended to be a way to save money. It was set up as a means for average people to try their hand at investing in the American Dream. Don't be afraid to invest in stocks, but only as a portion of your overall investment strategy. And become an informed investor before jumping in. Remember, you're investing in companies, not Wall Street. So do your homework and never invest money you can't afford to lose.

90 ⟩ MUTUAL FUNDS

Finding a good mutual fund is by far the best way to invest in the market with the least possible risk. It's also a way to easily diversify your investments with only a small amount of capital. Mutual funds are basically pools of money from hundreds and thousands of investors used to invest in a wide range of assets, including stocks, bonds, real estate, and other securities. And good mutual funds are managed by some of the best money managers in the country—people who you and I could never afford to hire on our own. The best thing about mutual funds is that they are categorized according to risk. You understand going in which ones are going to be high risk and which are going to be rather safe and boring. You decide your tolerance for risk and choose a mutual fund accordingly.

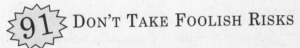

91 DON'T TAKE FOOLISH RISKS

It takes only one market crash for an investor to truly understand the importance of a diversified portfolio. For my wife and me, that lesson came in the crash of 2000. We had done so well picking stocks in the late 1990s that we were convinced we were a couple of financial whiz kids. So we started putting an inordinate amount of our investments in high-tech stocks. We couldn't lose! Until we lost. And trust me, we lost a chunk. A lot of others did as well, so we were not alone. The lesson we learned is a simple but important one: don't allow yourself to be fooled by a few good stock picks. Investing is a risky venture, and anything you can do to minimize that risk is a good idea. And that means learning and practicing the virtues of a well-diversified portfolio.

92 LEARN TO RECOGNIZE A SCAM

Once again, I speak from personal experience on this one. Some years ago we got taken in by a man who would buy and sell foreign currencies on the open market, just like most people bought and sold stocks. He had a three-year prospectus showing insane profits—more than 120 percent a year. So we jumped in and invested a sizable amount. Friends warned me to be careful—that if it sounds too good to be true, it probably is. But how do you argue with a written track record? You can't just make those things up, can you? Actually, you can, and he did. Within months his doors were closed, our money was gone, and he spent the next six years in prison. Learn how to recognize a scam if you want to protect your assets. It's the first rule of investing.

93 INVEST IN SMALL VENTURES

One of my good friends and business partners has developed quite a track record when it comes to investing in successful small businesses. He has dedicated a portion of his investment portfolio to be used as new venture capital—

meaning he helps fund new business ideas. Instead of simply loaning the money to people who want to go into business, he funds their start-up capital for a stake in the company. He invests only if he believes the venture will succeed and the person he's investing in can make it work. And he takes great care going over the business plan to make sure it's solid. Once invested, he keeps a close eye on his money by serving as a board member or consultant. This is a great option for someone who has a head for business and a reserve of cash ready to invest.

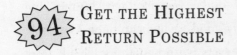 ## GET THE HIGHEST RETURN POSSIBLE

The starting place for any good investment is learning how to calculate your actual rate of return. A big mistake many investors make is simply looking at their monthly statements and assuming that the rate of return quoted is what they're actually getting. But there are lots of factors you don't see that need to be considered. When calculating your actual rate of return you have to consider hidden costs, like up-front fees charged by the broker, maintenance fees, annual fees, and other costs that might be added. There are also tax consequences you need to consider. All of these things need to be considered when calculating what your investments are actually netting you. Teach yourself how to calculate a true rate of return, and then use this formula before putting money in any type of mutual fund or other investment.

95 GET TO KNOW YOUR BANK MANAGER

This may sound strange, but it's another good business lesson I learned from my mother. She never ran a business, but she knew how to keep a good eye on her money. As a result, she knew the name of every person in our local bank, from the manager to the tellers—even the janitors. I don't go that far, but I do get to know the manager of every bank I do business with. If I have a problem I can call him directly to deal with it, instead of an 800 number somewhere in Calcutta. I can also make sure I'm getting the best prices and services on my accounts, as well as the best possible interest rates. This is a good practice for anyone wanting to maximize her saving and earning potential.

96 ⟩ NEVER INVEST BORROWED MONEY

This should go without saying, but you'd be surprised how many people ignore this simple principle of investing. Using borrowed money to invest is perhaps the greatest investing mistake a person can make. It's not only risky but makes it almost impossible to get a decent rate of return—simply because any amount you do make is offset by the interest you're paying on the borrowed money. This is why it's such a bad idea to invest money when you have high-interest loans hanging over your head. If you have the option to put $1,000 into a mutual fund or put it toward the balance of a 12 percent interest credit card, the decision should be an easy one. Pay down the balance of the card. If you don't, you're essentially investing with borrowed money, which is a horrible idea.

97 ⟩ SEEK ADVICE

When I need a toilet repaired, I call a plumber. When I need a room rewired, I call an electrician. When my car breaks down, I take it to a mechanic. All of these are things I could probably learn to do myself if I was willing to put in the time to learn. But instead I pay people who are trained and experienced in these things. The same holds true when it comes to investing. The best advice anyone can give you is to get good advice. It's as simple as that. Sometimes that means finding a trusted financial manager to handle your money. Other times it means attending seminars or reading books from proven financial experts. I mentioned Dave Ramsey earlier, and he's worth mentioning again, simply because he's the most no-nonsense financial advisor I know of. Seek solid advice and you'll be far ahead of the game.

98 BE GENEROUS

Money is not the root of all evil, but the love of money is. Anyone who loves money will never quite understand the joys of a giving spirit—nor the happiness that comes from being truly generous with what you have. Regardless of your financial goals or how you decide to go about increasing your family income, if they don't lead to a desire and ability to be more charitable, they are a waste of time and energy. Jesus said, "It is more blessed to give than to receive," and he wasn't necessarily talking about just an eternal blessing. Generous people live a more blessed existence, simply because they've put possessions in the right perspective. Make generosity your primary financial objective and you'll always be more successful—even if your net worth remains the same.

99 BE CONTENT

If you had to decide between happiness and success, what would you choose? Hopefully, most of us would choose to be happy. Thankfully, that's a choice you and I should never have to make, because these are not mutually exclusive ideals. Happiness is a state of the heart, not a measure of your bank account. Money is meaningless without a sense of personal joy and fulfillment. There's nothing wrong with wanting to increase your income—it's a great idea to be wise in how we use our time and resources. But never allow that to be your primary focus or your driving force. True contentment comes from learning to trust God in any situation, even when your 401(k) dwindles and your stocks crash. If you really want to be successful, let happiness and contentment be your primary goal. Then no economic downturn can ever keep you from truly succeeding at life!

PUTTING YOUR PLAN INTO ACTION

Wise financial choices can make all the difference when trying to earn extra income and increase your overall net worth. And wise choices begin by getting the right advice from the right people. Know your goals, and then find people who can help you reach them. Here again are the steps you should take when building a healthy financial portfolio:

- Set clear financial goals.
- Know the risks of stocks.
- Look for good no-load mutual funds.
- Minimize your risk.
- Don't be caught in a scam.
- Consider venture-capitalist opportunities.
- Know how to figure your rate of return.
- Get to know your banker.
- Don't invest borrowed money.
- Seek help.
- Give generously.
- Learn to be content with what you have.

More 99 Ways for
only $5.99!

99 Ways to Increase Your Income

Frank Martin

99 Ways to Stretch Your Home Budget

Cheri Gillard

99 Ways to Fight Worry and Stress

Elsa Kok Colopy

99 Ways to Entertain Your Family for Free

Mack Thomas

99 Ways to Build Job Security

Gary Nowinski

99 Bible Promises for Tough Times

Randy Petersen

In challenging times we all need advice on how to overcome stress and find encouragement. The 99 Ways books offer up-to-date, practical, and reliable information in a succinct format at a price anyone can afford.

WATERBROOK PRESS

www.waterbrookmultnomah.com